Collecting Fossils Between Whitby And Sandsend.

A Beginner's Guide.

James J. Browne.

Looking towards Whitby's piers.

Typical Whitby West Cliff scene.

James J. Browne.

COPYRIGHT© 20016.

James J. Browne and Samantha Browne.
The Cheese And Onion Doorstop Edition.

The attributed pictures by Alexander Vasenin and Didier Descouens are courtesy of the Creative Commons Attribution-Share Alike 4.0 International license.
Pictures by James J. Browne are copy-left for all purposes with the exception of advertisements for profit making organizations.

This book is not just licensed for your personal enjoyment only. This book may be re-sold or given away to other people. If you would like to share this book with another person, please purchase an additional copy for each recipient. This will enable our much cherished High Street book shops to remain with us for many years to come. Thank you for respecting the hard work of this author, the editors, proof readers, designers, printers, delivery men and book shop assistants who have brought it to you.

Please note that by buying your books from a High Street vendor, albeit sometimes at a higher price than online sellers, you are securing jobs and protecting the commercial heart of your community.

Atrox melior dulcissima veritas mendaciis.

What lies beneath the bedrock.

Introduction.

Within my limited experience, fossils seem to have the "marmite" factor. People either love or loathe them.

It was back in the late 1980's when I got into fossil collecting or, as it is known in scientific circles, paleontology. There was always something quite magical about finding ancient remains. Even now, it still amazes me, should I stumble upon a fossil during my travels, that I am most probably the first human being to see it for what it actually is! Finds can sometimes be very emotional experiences as they provide tangible evidence of our Earth's turbulent past. Mass extinctions, famines, climate change and huge meteor impacts are there within the fossil record for all to see.

Fear not! I shall not endeavor to bamboozle you with too many scientific terms or Latin names. I'll assume that you chose this book on this basis that it is "A Beginner's

Guide". I'll also assume that you have more than a passing interest in fossils and that you might wish to make your own collection.

Samantha laughed when I told her about the size of the fossil collection that I'd put together before I met her. I was never short of doorstops! However, my neighbors in the flat below lived in constant fear of a humongous rock fall coming through their ceiling.

Yours truly dug up a lot of stuff, mainly from around the Yorkshire coast. I had the pleasure of excavating an icthyosaur (a kind of Jurassic dolphin), a fair few plant fossils, fish, shrimps, sea urchins, seashells, ammonites (similar to the modern nautilus) and belemnites (a type of squid). I sold my most valuable specimens and donated a good bit of my collection to museums and schools. The rest ended up in a friend's rock garden.

Once I'd got rid of my collection, it was like I'd completed some kind of penance. Things you own can somehow end up owning you. Also, I've often suspected that collecting things is a little bit on the OCD side of the spectrum.

Nowadays, I just take photographs of the fossils I find. It's much easier and one's finds only amount to the weight of a camera at the end of the day. Intriguingly, this is not strictly true as digital data has weight too! (See http://www.cultofmac.com/299069/ipad-filled-apps-weighs-one-nothing-installed/)

As time went on, I realized that collecting fossils was not really my sole motivation for spending so much time by the sea. I was drawn to the shoreline because of the dynamics of the environment and how it made me feel about my place in it.

The seashore is never the same from one day to the next, the tides and the English weather make sure of that. At one moment you can be gazing at the tiny pebbles and creatures in a limpid rock pool, the next you can look out towards the crashing waves and feel dwarfed by the sheer scale of sea and the vastness of the sky above you.

Looking for fossils along a quiet stretch of beach can be very conducive to mindfulness. In an increasingly noisy world, the serenity of an open stretch of shore can often be a balm for troubled souls.

Before we start, one esoteric nugget of advice. *"If you go to the beach just looking for fossils, that'll be all you find."*

Sunset at Happy Valley.

James J. Browne.

Are there any fossils in this picture? Read the rest of the book then cast a more informed eye on it.
(The answer is at the very, very back of the book)

What you will need and safety stuff.

Presently, as I only have a small following, it would be a bit of a blow if I lost one of my readers through any advice, or lack of it, that I'd put in one of my books. Therefore, it would be most remiss of me if I did not provide you with the best advice I can muster. (Forgive me, but I feel a list coming on.)

What you will need.

Good strong waterproof boots that protect your ankles. These are essential if you are walking over lots of large shingle or rocky stretches of shoreline.

A brightly colored waterproof jacket (with hood). There's nothing to stop you taking a waterproof hat, I hate hoods myself but they are very convenient. The weather can change rapidly in England and it is quite easy to get hypothermia on exposed stretches of the North Yorkshire coast. If the heavens open and the wind turns north easterly it is possible for those who are unprepared to get into real trouble. If you want to be really safe take some **waterproof leggings** and make sure they're a lurid bright color.

A mobile phone for obvious reasons.

A light weight nylon rucksack with a plastic frame. Keeping weight down is most important as you will probably be walking for some distance. Also, you need to consider the fact that your rucksack will be much heavier later in the day. The plastic frame should save you from being struck by a thunderbolt during a storm. Waving a geological hammer above one's head during thunderstorms is not to be advised! I jest not. Do remember that during lightening storms one is especially vulnerable on open spaces such as beaches.

A good geological hammer. No! You can't use a domestic hammer and cold chisel. Geological hammers are made not to shatter or splinter when they hit hard rock, domestic ball or claw ended hammers aren't made for the job. Injuries from metal fragments are not pretty, which neatly leads me on to **protective goggles.** There is no excuse for not getting these, I've seen them on sale for less than a fiver and sometimes for as little as a pound.

A **first aid kit** would not go amiss. At some point, and I say this with no malicious intent, you will knock/injure your hand(s) with a lump of stone or your geological hammer.

A packed lunch with a warm drink. Who doesn't want to munch on a cheese and onion doorstop whilst wistfully gazing out to sea?

A friend to take with you. I don't wish to seem over dramatic, but there's safety in numbers, especially if you're a woman. Although, in all fairness, you'd be very unlucky to find a creep on a deserted stretch of shore. Invite an artist or someone with a dog – they'll really enjoy themselves and won't get under your feet.

<u>Safety stuff.</u>

Most of this is straightforward common sense stuff. Tell someone when and where you're going fossil collecting and, most importantly, what exact time they should start to worry. This'll save air and sea rescue a great deal of unnecessary aggravation.

CHECK THE TIDE TABLES!!!!!!!!!! You really wouldn't coco how many buffoons don't do this and end up stranded or...........................much worse! There's really no excuse.

Same goes for the weather forecast.

I stick to a general rule of thumb when I'm out on an unknown stretch of coast:

"If it doesn't look and feel safe, then it probably isn't safe."

Simple as that.

Getting one's eye in.

A typical melange of stones and pebbles. Fossil shells (centre) with an ammonite (directly underneath) showing its white calcite inner chambers.

The last chapter talked about the equipment you will need when you go out collecting. Importantly, we also talked about safety!!!!!!

In this chapter we'll talk about what you might expect to find and the skills you'll need.

When I used to go out with Fossil Shop Dave we used to jokingly ask each other - "Have you got your eye in?" A good pair of eyes goes a long way but, first of all, you need to know what you're looking for.

So let us begin...........................

The stretch of shoreline between Whitby and Sandsend is a veritable cornucopia for the newcomer to fossils. It's also the paleontologists equivalent to the nursery slopes and is one of the safest places for collecting in the England. One would have to make a dedicated effort to become cut off on this bit of coastline.

Before you say, "a chap at the bed and breakfast told me to go to the Whitby East Cliff", I shall tell you why you shouldn't.

Firstly, whilst it is true you will find lots of fossils in the shale cliffs, you run the risk of being hit by falling rocks.

Secondly, fossil collecting that involves chiseling at the cliffs or bedrock is frowned upon. The East Cliff is a site of scientific interest and enthusiastic hammer wielding amateurs are not encouraged.

Thirdly, the fossils you will find are likely to disintegrate faster than a bunch of flowers from a pound shop. Shale does not stand the test of time once it is exposed to the air.

Marvel at the wonders of the East Cliffs, take a few photos, but don't contribute to their already frightening rate of erosion with your geology hammer. It's by far the safest and most environmentally friendly option.

Ammonites, Whitby's classic fossil.

Most visitors to Whitby would like to find an ammonite, and it is possible to easily do so on the West Cliff beach.

Ammonites, by the way, were tentacled predators and possessed ribbed spiral-form shells like the ones in our picture. Their bodies were not unlike those of squids. However, it is rare to find an ammonite in its complete form as the soft body decomposed much more rapidly than the hard shell. These creatures lived in tropical seas about 250 million years ago and became extinct at the end of the Cretaceous period. The name 'ammonite' originates from the Egyptian Ram-horned god called Ammon. Their living relatives include the octopus, squid, cuttlefish and nautilus.

Ammonites moved by expelling water through a small opening near their tentacles – a sort of underwater jet propulsion. They are believed to have only had a two year lifespan, palaeontologists estimated this through close studies of the ammonites living relatives. Modern day nautilus' possess many characteristics similar to those of the ammonites.

Some ammonite fossils bear intricate patterns on their outer surface and these are are often visible if the fossil has been subject to weathering or artificial polishing. These patterns mark where the walls of the ammonite's inner chambers meet the outer wall of the shell.

A clump of belemnites - note the bullet shape just below center left.

Belemnites, also known as "Devil's Thunderbolts", were numerous during the Jurassic period and became extinct at the end of the Cretaceous period. They are often found side by side with their cousins, the ammonites. Normally, with fossil belemnites, only the bullet-shaped back part of the shell (called the guard or rostrum) is found.

If you find something washed up with shingle and stones that resembles a stone bullet, or a small stem, then you've probably found a belemnite. As often as not, you will find them in clumps (see picture on left) or in the same stone as other fossils. The modern day relatives of the "Devil's Thunderbolt" include octopus, squid, cuttlefish and the nautilus.

Fossil shells – including oyster and pectin shells.

Once you "get your eye in" you will

literally buckle under the weight of your fossil seashell finds. These are going to be some of the prettiest finds you'll make and you can take them home with the clearest of consciences. Fossils found washed up on the beach are of little scientific interest. However, specimens found in situ can tell a paleontologist all manner of wondrous things.

Gryphea or "Devil's toenails".

One of the commonest fossil seashells is the gryphea, an ancient type of oyster. These can be found plentifully between Whitby and

Sandsend, either in boulders or singly.

A single "Devil's toenail" (actual size). This one has been smoothed by sea action. Often these shells are found in a good state of preservation with ridges on them like modern oysters.

Fossil coral is also abundant. Sadly, I've always found the best specimens in unbreakable and immovable boulders.

Fossil corals look little different from their living relatives – I suppose some natural designs just can't be improved upon. Corals are animals but, rather strangely, they make themselves a calcium carbonate skeleton that looks similar to rock. They also have a symbiotic relationship with plant-like cells called zooxanthellae.

The zooxanthellae live in the soft tissue of a coral polyp and use

21

sunlight to photosynthesize and create a by-product that the coral can use as food. A pay off is that the coral provides the zooxanthellae with shelter and nutrients.

Corals also capture food with stinging tentacles and catch the microscopic organisms that float in the water. Corals are native to warm shallow waters that receive plenty of light.

A piece of fossil coral.

Crinoids, or sea lilies, are common attractive fossil finds and like corals they also have living relatives.

Crinoids – individual sections of the stem of this creature look like beads. Crinoid sections are also known as "St Cuthbert's beads" and were often used to make rosaries.

Crinoids are marine animals and their name comes from the Greek word krinon, "a lily", and eidos, "form". They have been found in shallow water but can also be seen at depths as great as 30,000 ft.

These lovely members of the echinoderm family are characterized by a mouth on their top surface that is surrounded by feeding arms. They have, interestingly enough, a U-shaped gut which dictates that their anus is next to their mouth, yum! Although the basic echinoderm pattern is five arms evenly spaced, most crinoids have in excess of that. They usually have a stem which they use to attach themselves to the sea bed. However, many become free-swimming as adults.

Present day crinoid (photo by Alexander Vasenin).

Presently, there are only about 600 crinoid species. The fossil record shows that they were certainly much more abundant and diverse in the past. This is borne out by the existence of thick limestone beds, dating to the mid to late Paleozoic, made up of disarticulated crinoid fragments.

Fossil leaf (photo by Didier Descouens).

Palaeobotany (from the Greek words paleon meaning "old" and "botany", study of plants) is the scientific branch of fossil collecting which deals with the recovery and identification of plant remains. It is an ideal occupation for someone who has a good working knowledge of contemporary botany.

You'll be very lucky to come upon a find such as the one shown in the photo above, especially on the beach north of Whitby harbor. In fact, you'll be very fortunate if you find anything truly resembling a plant. Most of the plant fossils here, usually found in sandstone or shale, will be mere strands of crumbly black carbon. On the odd occasion, you might stumble upon a fossil log. These are quite intriguing as you can often see, in cross section, the yearly rings of the plant from the time it was alive. Needless to say, fossil logs are heavy finds.

Plant fossils from Whitby beach. There are traces of black carbon on the specimen on the left. The pitting and lines on the other specimen is where the carbon remains of plants has been washed away by the action of the sea.

One plant fossil you can easily find, with a little patience, is the semi-precious stone known as Whitby Jet. Jet, when polished, takes on an intense luster of opaque black, this gave rise to the term 'jet-black'`. Its rich black color never diminishes and the shine is such that polished jet was used to make mirrors in medieval times.

Jet is an unusually pure and hard form of fossilized wood and is the remains of a once abundant ancient species of monkey puzzle tree.

In its rough form, jet occurs as thin lens-shaped seams within the shale rocks surrounding Whitby. These "jet rocks" were laid down in the early Jurassic era some 175-185 million years ago.

Most sea washed jet looks a bit like lumps of broken black plastic. It's very light in weight and takes on the heat of your hand very quickly. To test your piece of jet, just chalk it on a bit of sandstone. Genuine jet, despite being black in color, leaves a brown mark. If what you've found leaves a black mark, then you've found another type of plant fossil – sea coal! Folklore has it that such a find will bring good fortune to its bearer.

The fossils you will find on the Whitby to Sandsend beach are the result of erosion and the wave actions that transported them to the beach. Consequently, you are not going to find a whole dinosaur. In fact fossil bone finds of any kind are quite unusual. You may find the odd bone or tooth fragment amongst the shingle or rocks, but it will be nigh on impossible to identify exactly what creature it came from. For the purposes of identification, fossil bone looks very like normal bone – it's pretty much unmistakable.

An icthyosaur skeleton, carved into the west pier by Darren Yeadon.

It is possible to find fossil fish, sea urchins, crabs and shrimps. However, such finds are rare and, generally speaking, you are more likely to find fragments rather than a complete creature. Sorry about that!

James J. Browne.

Can you spot the fossils?

"Getting your eye in" takes time and patience, in that respect fossil collecting is like a lot of things in life. As the mystical Chinese "I Ching" says – *Perseverance furthers.*

Sandsend from the sea defenses.

<u>Fossil Jokes.</u>
(Best left buried in my opinion.)

In twenty million years time Paleontologists will dig up tanning beds and think we fried people as punishment.

Why are there old dinosaur bones in the museum?
Because they can't afford new ones!

What did the pokemon trainer say when it told the pterodactyl to fly?
Dino, saur!

Whitby to Sandsend.

Our starting point - west pier slipway.

Before we begin, you'll be pleased to know that there is a good bus service in this area. You can either set off from Whitby or Sandsend and catch the X4 bus home. Alternatively, you can walk from Whitby to Sandsend and then back again. It's not an overly long walk and would take, there and back, about three or four hours at a dawdle.

At this point I'm assuming you've checked the tide times and are suitably equipped for the weather.

There are two types of fossil collectors, the tortoise and the hare. The hare will dash around looking frantically in all directions. The tortoise does the exact opposite and settles for one patch of rocks, which they comb thoroughly, before moving on. Generally speaking, tortoises make better collectors than hares. Remember, you're not in a race! Besides, don't you want to take in something of the atmosphere of this impressive bit of shoreline.

Normally, I'd find a rocky spot and mooch around, sometimes it takes a few minutes to "get your eye in". A lot of collectors miss the following point – some of your best finds will often be no bigger than a child's fist. Look through the shingle and pebbles as well as the rocks!

On a decent day, the walk from Whitby to Sandsend is a delight. It's best to collect on this stretch out of season as the tides are rougher due to the weather. More debris is thrown onto the beach in the winter months and during the high spring and autumn tides.

Once you've walked past the Spa Pavillion you get more of a feel of being out in the natural world. Eventually, the sea wall runs out at a spot called Happy Valley.

The fossils pictured below are what I found on a gentle jaunt between Whitby and Happy Valley.

Finds on Whitby beach – six ammonites, some fossil shells (centre) and a sea urchin (top left).

The fossil sea urchin is a bit of a red herring. I found it in a pile of limestone rubble that had been abandoned by builders on the cliff path leading out of Happy Valley.

As an aside, the cliff path which bears left from near the top of Happy Valley (just before the bridge) leads up to a short track on the cliff top just at the edge of the golf course. Once you reach here you're not too far from Whitby's best kept secret, The White House. You'll get a good pint and the fish and chips are definitely amongst the best you'll eat in this area. Just follow the track by the golf course to the fork in the road and proceed by taking the right hand prong. Walk about a further hundred yards or so and The White House is on the right.

Can you spot the fossils?

Remember, once you "get your eye in" you'll see fossils everywhere. I'll never forget my amazement when I saw fossil corals in the polished stone of the columns of Durham Cathedral. After that, I couldn't help myself from looking for fossil remains in the stonework of our numerous public buildings.

You'll see that three of the ammonites I found look like they've been hit with a hammer. You can see the jagged rock. Strangely enough, I found them like that. Chances are these were dropped by a collector who wasn't too impressed with what they'd found.

The best preserved ammonites come in nodules. These are often called concretions because they are like concrete and, indeed, concrete can be made from them. Nodules come in all shapes and sizes and some of the larger types of ammonite can be found in nodules a foot in diameter.

You'll often find a little bit of a an ammonite peeping out from a nodule. In most cases this will be the edge of its ribbed shell, sometimes you'll see the glisten of the white calcite within it if it has been well washed by the sea.

A typical none starter (see if you found this in the top picture on page 29). Note the large crack on the underside.

There's a knack to opening ammonites. First thing is to recognize when you've got a none starter.

If a nodule rings when you hit it with your hammer, then forget it! You'll break your arm before you break the nodule. Look before you whack, are there lots of cracks in your nodule like there are in the one above? It saves a lot of wasted effort.

It's best to try and open nodules while you're on the beach, this will save you some disappointment and lower the load in your rucksack. In all honesty, you'll probably wreck a good few dozen nodules before you get the hang of opening them.

One whack with a hammer and our none starter is in bits. Nice cast on the left though!

The picture below is a much more promising prospect.

You can see from the crack on the top of the nodule exactly where I've hit it. Again, take the time to examine a nodule before you blithely whack it one! A single hammer blow on a well spotted crack, or weak spot, can often effortlessly reveal the finest of specimens.

And there you go! One ammonite complete with its cast.

Once you arrive at Sandsend you

can take a break at one of its many excellent cafés. The cliffs beyond the stream that cuts through the village will look tempting. Don't bother, yours truly has collected around there. I can assure you there isn't much to be found and you'll run a really good chance of being cut off by the tides.

There are fossils in all of these pictures. Can you find them?

Holding your own.

It's surprising what one finds on the beach.

At some point, whilst you are out and about collecting, someone will sidle up to you and ask what you are up to. If you make the foolish mistake of saying you're out hunting for fossils then you'll deserve every question you get!

In the highly likely event of this happening, I have written this chapter to help you to "hold your own" and not appear to be a complete numpty. This will be useful when talking to other fossil collectors and inquisitive kids.

The following list is a concise collection of quotable fossil facts and only the most "hardcore" (love the pun) of fossil enthusiasts will have pursued studies beyond these basic bits of information.

Paleontology is the study the forms of life that existed in former geologic periods through the scrutiny of fossils. Fossils can be found on every continent on Earth.

Fossils are the remains of ancient animals and plants. They are also the traces, or the traces of their activities, or impressions of living things from past geologic ages.

The word fossil comes from, you guessed it, the Latin word fossilis, which means, "dug up". The majority of fossils are excavated from sedimentary rock layers such as sand, mud, and small bits of rock. After considerable time, these small pieces of debris are compressed and are buried under more layers of sediment. The incrementally increased weight of the sediment, over time, means that the debris and anything in it will be compressed into sedimentary rock.

A fossil bone doesn't have any bone in it! A fossilized object keeps its shape unless subjected to extreme pressure, but chemically is more like a rock.

Petrification can preserve both hard and soft parts of creatures and slowly replaces organic material with silica, calcite or pyrite, forming a rock-like fossil. Interestingly ancient wood is often found in petrified form.

Some organisms, such as insects or plants, are embedded in Amber (a hardened form of tree sap).

In the right circumstances imprints,

such as dinosaur footprints, fill with sediments that fossilize.

Very few creatures fossilize, they simply decay and are lost forever. Paleontologists estimate that the merest fraction of the dinosaurs that ever lived have been, or will be, found as fossils.

You probably won't need to share more than a fraction of this info. Fortunately, most people swiftly start to glaze over and allow you continue with the fascinating business of rooting around amongst the rocks.

"Get your eye in, hold your own, and know that If you go to the beach just looking for fossils, that'll be all you find."

Fossils and a good yarn.

The North Sea and Whitby's Piers - a big sea with big skies.

If you've managed to get so far into this book, then I'm pretty much certain that your imagination is at least a little inspired by fossils and what they represent.

In themselves, fossils can be deadly dull. They are, to some extent, merely a colorless representation or shadow of something that once lived. For those enthusiasts who want to engage the uninterested, fossils are a hard sell.

There are three ways you can go

after reading this book. The first is that you'll put this volume down and never really think much about fossils again. Some of you will go out collecting a few times, learn a bit about fossils, but never feel a passion for the subject. The third way will lead you down to the path of being an enthusiast and you'll end up with a house full of rocks, just like I did back in the eighties.

At some point a friend, or guest, might notice a specimen you have on display and politely inquire about it. Before you consider doing your very best David Attenborough impression, may I suggest a different approach. We don't want your guest/friend to end up staring blankly back at you, for a few brief uncomfortable moments, before they nod off.

By all means tell them what the fossil is, that makes sense. But, and it's a big but, remember that just as there aren't many good fossil jokes (see page 30) there aren't many exceptional fossil yarns either. It's up to you to make them up.

Tell them about where you found the fossil and don't be afraid to bull up your tale a little. Everyone's ears prick up if a hint of danger, or something supernatural, is brought into a tale. Is that not so?

To make your life, and your story of fossil daring do, easier I've added a few folk tales connected with the specimens you might find between Whitby and Sandsend. The danger bit, you can add that yourselves. Here goes..........

As you know, ammonites are very commonly found fossils in Britain and their folklore is largely Christian in origin. They were trumpeted as "snakestones" by the early Christians and these snakestones were unashamedly used as evidence to back up stories of snakes being cast out by Christian saints. No doubt ammonites were used to illustrate the stories of St Hilda, the Saxon abbess of Whitby, who drove away all the snakes before building an abbey, and

St Patrick of Ireland – which now has no native snakes. Snakes and serpents are considered to have devilish connotations, hence the necessity of casting them out before building on a sacred place. It was not uncommon for the heads of snakes to be carved on ammonites to help further propagate the legends connected with them.

Ammonites are also known as "Druid's Eggs" and are believed to have the power to relieve headaches.

The thick and curving shells of gryphea are not dissimilar to malformed toenails. The twisted shape of these fossils also resembles arthritic joints. Gryphea, or "Devil's Toenails" were used to cure joint pain, using the sympathetic medicine approach of like curing like.

Other names for these fossils include "Crouching Stones", "Cuckoo Shells" and "Milner's Thumbs". Powdered Milner's thumbs, according to the diary of Abraham de la Pryme of the 10th April 1696, could cure the sore back of a horse in less than three days.

Belemnites look rather like Lee Enfield .303 bullet tips. In the Middle Ages, when fields in the Norfolk chalk and Oxford clay were turned over, heavy rain or a thunderstorm would wash the clay and chalk away leaving only the belemnites that had been hidden in these soft deposits. This inevitably lead to the myth that they were thunderbolts. Belemnites are also known as "St Peter's Fingers", "Devil's Fingers" and, rather bizarrely, "Ghostly Candles".

When resin seeped out of ancient trees, its stickiness frequently trapped insects and other small creatures. When the resin fossilized to become amber the organisms within it appeared to be perfectly preserved.

Michael Crichton, the author of Jurassic Park, helped to perpetrate the myth that it is possible to extract dinosaur DNA from the last blood-meal of a prehistoric mosquito trapped in amber.

The truth is, any DNA that survived in amber would be so damaged that it would be impossible to recreate anything, let alone dinosaurs, from it. Steven Spielberg didn't let the science get in the way of him making a mint when he made the astonishingly successful movie of Crichton's book in 1993.

Whilst on the subject of fossil tree resin, Whitby Jet is believed to have the power to ward off serpents if kept in one's pocket. It also has the ability to ward off demons when burnt.

I'd like to wish you the very best of luck with all your future fossil collecting adventures. I also hope you will craft many positive memories and ripping yarns from them.

Happy hunting – James J. Browne.

All the fossils photographed in this book were collected by Browne in the space of one long afternoon. This was done to give as fair a representation as possible of what the reader might find for themselves in the same time period.

All the photographs by James J Browne used in this book can be supplied (for non commercial purposes) on request.

Email:florunhouse@gmail.com

Fossil shells in a boulder near Sandsend.

James J. Browne (1962-) has managed to survive for over 50 years whilst having had many diverse and not necessarily interesting occupations. He has been, prior to leaving Blighty, a professional musician, a tour guide, road sweeper, recycling operative, telephone fortune teller, insulation installation operative, light bulb packer, antique dealer, waiter, sea shell salesman and barman to name but a few.

James is also a graduate in Art History and a qualified EFL teacher. It was his brief career as a taxi driver, during the Crash, that decided it was time for him to leave England behind. His work as a château guardian in France inspired him to write "The Three Grand Brits".

He has maintained a life long interest in all things considered supernatural and incorporates these into his written work. He started to read palms and the tarot during his early teens and was giving professional readings at the age of sixteen. He makes no secret of the fact he has bipolar disorder.

Presently, he lives and travels with his long suffering partner Samantha and two golden retrievers in a Fiat Ducato.

Dedicated to "Fossil Shop Dave" - I wish we'd talked more when we had chance to.

James J. Browne.

Yes! The fossils are the white semi circles in the gray rock in the middle. It contains seashell fragments. The dark blue and black part of the rock is most probably the remains of marine vegetation.

12325839R00030

Printed in Great Britain
by Amazon